I'M JUST SAYING: YOU DON'T HAVE TO AGREE!
WRITTEN BY RITA U. MCCAIN

EDITED BY NADINE MCNEAL, LMSW

Copy right date- August 8, 2014
©1-1646931941
Contact information-
Phone 731-988-6245
Fax 731-989-6838
FINALLY A CHANCE
Henderson, TN 38340-0704
Askmeanything731.wix.com/finallyachance

## MY PRAYER

Lord,

I want to thank you for every word on these pages; it is all inspired by You. Thank you for thinking enough of me, to use me to do Your will. Thank you for the good Christian education You gave me the strength to see through. It was because of You humbling me, that I was in the right position to receive it. Most of all, thank you for saving me. Lord, I ask that every person, who reads the words on these pages, develops a desire to get closer to You.

In the precious name of Jesus, I pray

AMEN

## INTRODUCTION

I'M JUST SAYING; YOU DON'T HAVE TO AGREE, is a collection of articles that I published in the local weekly newspaper. An article was published about once a month. These short articles are about real life situations that all people encounter from time to time. It is an easy read, because I wanted to make it easy to understand. Issues addressed include marriage, relationships with various people, bullying, and so much more.

I hope this will be helpful information that you can relate to your own life to help it be more manageable. The Spirit within me inspires all my work. It does not matter what I think this book should be about; I could not have brought it together without my Help from above.

I hope this will inspire you to keep pressing forward, stay encouraged, and keep it moving!

## TABLE OF CONTENT

### Getting It All In……

Do you sometimes find yourself spinning out of control, wishing you could clone yourself, just so you can be in all the places you want to be? Well dream on, because it ain't gonna happen!

You have to know if your life is out of control by choice or force. If it's by force, then ask yourself, "Is it worth it?" I mean, let's face it, we're all "grown folks", and the best part of being "grown" is not being forced to do anything we don't want to do! We should all live by choice. But, what determines the choices we make? Should the kids come before the job? Where does the relationship fit in- after the kids, but before the job or vice versa? Is it more important for you to be happy or everybody else?

Who's not just a little crazy? Just thinking about juggling work, kids, relationships, family, finances and anything else from A to Z that can happen in the course of the day is enough to drive anybody crazy! How you deal with everyday situations determine just how crazy you will be. Keeping things in perspective will not only help you better manage, but most importantly, it will alleviate some unnecessary stress.

There is no perfect order for everybody. But I will share with you what works for me. I keep my God first then MYSELF second. Now, if that sounds selfish, well too bad. If I had not begun putting myself before my family and everyone else in 2000, I may not be around to talk about it now. In any decision I've made since 1988, I have always taken the best interest of my children into consideration. Not that they liked the decisions, but that's the good thing about being the parent.

I made choices for them, keeping in mind that they would eventually be grown and I don't do unnecessary stress. We all need a certain amount of stress to keep us on our toes, but enough is enough!

Imagine this-Controlling your kids at any age; learning how to tolerate your job; finding financial peace; or really communicating with your mate- It Can Happen.

**Remember: To your own self, always be true.**

## Who's Really in Control ????

Children (gotta lov'em) are our future; and right now, it's not looking very bright. What happened? The majority of us, who were born before 1970, knew what it meant to get our butts beat not out in the streets, but at home, by those who loved and cared for us the most, our parents! Most of us were scared to get into trouble at school or away from home. Scared of whom- our parents! We were taught respect for our parents and the home they provided us. Likewise, we were taught respect for our neighbors, as well as ourselves. We were held accountable for our actions.

If you grew up with hand me downs, then you were glad when Easter or your birthday rolled around because you were able to get something new to wear. If you had chores to do on Saturday morning, they were done, without question. They were done right the first time, because you knew the consequences if they were not. If your parents asked you a question, you gave an answer. If you were being yelled at, you kept your mouth shut; talking back was just not accepted. For the most part, we turned out all right. So what happened? Why do we accept less from our own children?

It was not always easy for our parents to maintain a little fear in our heart, to keep us on the right path. Of course, we kept them on their toes with a little mischief from time to time, but we knew how far to go. But for the most part, our parents held firm, did what they had to do, and then- when you ready, they set us free. Some of us had to stumble, slip, slide, and roll before we finally gained our footing and found our own paths. But during those times, we were constantly hearing familiar voices in our ears from our parents, teachers, church members, neighbors, and all who had a part in making us the people we are today. What will your children hear as they try to find their way from childhood to adulthood?

Our parents did the best they could with what they knew how. Now since we know better, we can do better. Who knows better what awaits your children in this cold cruel world better than YOU? Let's keep it real- you've been there, done that, and invented most of it! Tell your children what's waiting for them out there, so when it comes to them (and it will), they will not be caught off guard. Children are never too young to learn life's lessons.

Life lessons come with age, just like school. The number one lesson: discipline, must begin in infancy. A screaming baby grows into a whining fussy infant. This infant grows into a temper tantrum -throwing toddler. He continues to grow into a defiant, spoiled adolescent. Then over night, he grows into a rude and disrespectful teenager. Lastly, becomes an out of control adult.

When people reach the age of 18, they are legally considered adults. Throughout childhood, if they are shown love, kept safe, and provided with their basic needs, they will become adults who love themselves, are trustworthy, and know what is needed to survive. Be sure to show encouragement every chance you get; it builds self-esteem and self-worth. Children should work for what they want. A child who learns how to work has a better chance of becoming an adult who knows how to work. If children are held accountable for their actions, they will learn consequences. Let them know the consequences at age 10 or 12, may be a simple punishment or, if necessary, a beating. Realize the consequences as they get older could mean jail, an unwanted pregnancy, or worse. Consequences for their actions when young will give them something to think about when it comes times to make hard choices. Will they always make the right choice? Did you? Think about it; they should be better armed than you were, and thus make better choices.

Loving your children is more than just providing basic and material possessions. Talk to your children, and most important, listen! Do not let them cut you out of their lives, because you will catch hell trying to get back in. Remember, they learn more from your actions than your words. So, set good examples.

Now here's the catch-You have 18 years to do it. When they get about 14-15 years old, it dawns on them that they will not have to do what you say for the rest of their lives, just until they turn 18 or you kick them out; which ever comes first! Oh and the other catch, you have to wait until they reach that age, to find out if they were listening. You only have 18 years, because you cannot raise an adult!

One of my favorite sayings to my kids: If I can't teach it to you in 18 years, then the SCHOOL OF HARD KNOCKS is holding class every day, and it has room for you!

# CAN U MAKE A DIFFERENCE?

As we began a new school year, I was compelled to address a few issues concerning parents, students, teachers, and administrators. This is strictly MY opinion and if it helps one person, then it will be well worth it.

**Parents:**

Charity (love) begins at home. Children are allowed to attend public school because it is their constitutional right to an education. However, when school time is disrupted because a teacher has to spend time getting a child to behave, this robs other students of their right to an education. I have told my children before, "If you want to sit there and do nothing, then that's your choice, but you better not be there acting a fool and stop others from learning." School is for acquiring knowledge and development of social skills that will help one succeed in the next phase of life. PLEASE let your children know- SCHOOL IS NOT AN OPTION; IT IS THE LAW! There are consequences for disruptive behavior while at school; if you- the parent do not want your child to be disciplined by the people in charge of their education, then you have two choices: raise them with discipline and respect for school personnel, all adults, and the other students, or home school them. If home schooling is not an option, and your child is having problems at school, address it with the proper authorities until there is a resolution. PLEASE do not say what your child (or anybody) will or will not do; it can save you from a severe let down later.

**Students:**

There is no such thing as the perfect family. While some are fortunate to come from a two-parent household, with a good income and the ability to provide all their wants and needs, it does not mean this is the case for all your schoolmates. There is not one child at school who is any better than the other; every student is just as good as the next. As children, you are not responsible for how or where you live, what you do or do not have. This is the responsibility of the person who is legally responsible for you as a minor.

Our world is a "melting pot". It is made of different people from a lot of different places, with the same goal: To live the best they can with what they have and to have more. No student has the right to make fun of or belittle another student. Regardless of what you see on the outside, we are all the same. Everyone has feelings-just like you. You feel hurt or upset if someone says something negative about you, this is also true of the person you choose to treat in a negative way. If for some reason you feel you are better than the next person, you are wrong: You only have what you have because your parents or the people responsible for your upbringing give it to you. There is an episode of the Cosby show where Vanessa gets into a fight, because after telling some of her class mates how much her parents paid for a painting, they teased her for being a "rich girl". She asks her dad, why they had to be rich, he politely informed her, "You are not rich; your mother and I are-YOU have nothing!"

Treat all people how you want to be treated. Some things have NO place at school. Things like Face Book, Instagram, texting and any other social media is done outside of school and that's where they need to stay. Your main reason for going to school is to learn; if these things were part of the educational process, there would be room for it in the curriculum. I personally feel like no student should be allowed to have a cell phone at school-for what? Your parents know where you are and can call the school if they need to reach you, and you can use the phone in the office if you need to reach them. Anything else, has it's own time-AFTER school.

**Teachers and Administrators:**

If you are in the field of education because you could not get a decent job with your undergraduate degree, and you figured you would take a few more classes and become a teacher; you need to find another job. Teaching requires a deep desire to see ALL students succeed; regardless of race, nationality or social-economic background. If you encounter a student that seems to have a problem, don't be afraid to privately ask them if there is anything YOU can do to help (discussing it with others who have no knowledge of the situation probably won't help much). Contact the parent or guardian and see if there is something you may need to know to better help understand what may be going on. There are some parents who do not have the luxury to attend every parent-teacher conference, or be a member of the booster club or overly involved because they are focused on providing the basic necessities for their family. There could be an unstable home life or a single parent or grandparent that is doing the best they can with their [own] circumstances. Don't assume they don't care; instead-get the facts. Teachers and administrators sometime spend more time with some students than their parents; take advantage of this opportunity to be the **encouragement** this child needs in order to succeed. If the students notice a child has a hygiene problem, then you should too. Taking the time to pull this child to the side or send them to the counselor and address the problem, will go a whole lot further than ignoring it and watching them being ridiculed by the others. I am certain all of you are way over twenty-one, so don't be afraid to step out of your comfort zone in order to make a difference in the life of a child. Also, make it a habit to leave your personal problems in your car, and not bring them into school with you. This is unfair to the students, because they are being robbed of the time and attention that has been designated just for them.

I have never had the desire to become a schoolteacher; I do not have what it takes to deal with children who are not raised with discipline and respect; the ABC's would go straight out the window, because in my opinion, without discipline and respect, an education will not go very far. I have worked in the healthcare/helping profession all my adult life and I have a high regard for anyone who has chosen to take on this so very honorable profession of teaching. However, I am a parent with two children that have been in the Public School system, and one with a year left. I have always told them: "We may not have as much as some, but we do have more than others". And, "You know what you come home to at the end of the day, but you don't have a clue of what goes on in the home of some of your school mates. When I was not able to get them something they wanted-"That's why you need to finish school, get a good education and a good job, so you can buy yourself all those little things momma won't get you". And my favorite, "The law says I have to feed you, cloth you, educated you and provide a roof over your head; anything else is out of the goodness of my heart!!!!

**LABELS:  It's Not What You're Called;
BUT What You Answer To**

There is a big difference between a title and a label; titles
are what you do (parent, teacher, president, supervisor....etc....);
labels (bad, lazy, hyper, fast, mischievous, Christian, etc....) are
what other people think of you based on their perception of who
they think you are. Titles are earned; labels are given. One needs
to careful what "label" one puts on another person, and even some
of the labels one puts on them self.  Please be cautious when you
decide to put a "label" or "title" on another person without all the
facts.

To call a child "bad", or a young lady "fast", or a person
"stupid" or "lazy" or "good for nothing" without all the facts, can
become a self-fulfilling prophecy if the person hears it often
enough or from people they trust and respect. While negative
labels are not good; positive labels come with their own set of
problems. Positive labels can put unnecessary pressure on an
individual; they can drive themselves crazy trying to live up to
what other people think they should be. I personally think it is
easier to live up to a positive label, than to lower one's self to the

negative labels given by someone else. Most people do what will get them the most attention. Young ladies that are called "fast" or young men called "mannish" may try to live up to this name because it gets them attention from the opposite sex or attention from peers who can only see the outside; thinking, "Wow, I want to be like that". It can also get them attention they crave from parents or other adults; "If the only time you will pay attention to me is when I act up; then, I will take what I can get".

A person (young or old) who is labeled in a negative way, but gets what he or she wants (negative behavior=positive outcome) will continue with this type of behavior, because people convince themselves this is how to get what they want. However, these types of behaviors always end in a bad way, because eventually you will have to answer to others who "don't have a dog in your fight"; in other words, they don't care how you feel; you will conform to societal norms or suffer the consequences. Parents, family, or friends may be accommodating to this behavior because they don't want you to be angry or upset. This is setting the individual up to fail. While they may care how you feel-others won't and you will eventually become handicapped, because you never had to "play nice with others" to get along.

Negative labels like alcoholic, drug addict, convict, abuser, "loose", or womanizer do not describe the person, but rather the actions or behavior of the individual. What if the alcoholic was given his first drink when he was five or six, because someone thought the effects were cute or funny? But at ten or eleven, they started to sneak in the liquor cabinet because they wanted to be cute or funny, then as an adult because they wanted to be cute and funny. Only now, the affects are obnoxious or abusive (not cute or funny).

What if the drug addicts or convicts were left to raise themselves because the person responsible for their upbringing left them to fend for themselves as children, because they were too busy doing their own thing to care? This person grows up in "survival mode" and all they know is how to survive-good or bad, as long as the end results meets their need. What if the "loose woman" or womanizing man was sexually abused as a child which started them on a path that physically, mentally, and emotionally took a life of its own from that day forward? They don't know why, but they know there is something in them that needs to be fulfilled and sex is a temporary fix. The first step to solving a problem is first admitting there is a problem.

Let us be careful what "labels" we put on other people. And, let us be careful of the "labels" we live up to. The only label or title I want put on me, is that of a Christian. There is only one person who really knows if I live up to it, because He who searches the mind, also knows the heart. People see what you do; but only God knows why we do it!!!

**Remember, IT'S NOT WHAT YOU'RE CALLED, BUT WHAT YOU ANSWER TO!**

# Be VICTORIUS- Not A VICTIM

Encarta Dictionary
**Bully**- an aggressive person who intimidates or mistreats weaker people.
**Bullying**- intimidating or mistreating a weaker person.
**Intimidate**- 1. Persuade or dissuade by frightening; to frighten somebody into doing or not doing something, e.g. by means of violence or blackmail
      2. Daunt- to create a feeling of fear, awe, or inadequacy in another person
**Self-esteem**- Self –respect; confidence in your own merit as an individual
**Self-worth**- Confidence in personal value and worth as an individual person

It really saddens me to hear of all the things going on in our schools; and in some instances in our homes, that concerns the raising, discipline, and accountability towards those entrusted in our care. All children are a blessing from God, who gives special kids to special people. If your child seems healthy, happy and safe; be thankful. Children that know they are loved, secured, and raised with established boundaries grow up with a sense of security not only in themselves, but also with value and worth as a person (self-esteem; self-worth). Without boundaries, kids grow up with a sense of entitlement, rebellion, and total disrespect. If your children do not have respect for the person who cares and provides for them, they will have an extremely hard time showing respect to others. Kids do not always do what you say; but sometimes, they do what you do.

## Please share the following with a young person you know.

All people are made to be different; every last one of us is special in our own way. Have you ever considered that every person older than you had to once be your age in order to get there? Unfortunately for you, the world has changed and so have some of the people along with it. This will be the world, as you know it. Now, don't get me wrong, I like to believe that there is much more kindness and goodness in the world than bad, but it is the bad that one must learn to deal with in order to succeed.

We all have feelings, and nobody wants his or her feelings hurt. What one considers "speaking her mind" can actually be really hurtful to another person? When comments are made because of what one sees on the outside, they can cut a person deeply, depending on what they are dealing with on the inside. There are some people that do not feel good about themselves or their life circumstances; some not even knowing why, but they take it out on others, sometime without even realizing it. Frustration, anger, and resentment are all unleashed on people who choose to take it.

FYI: The only people who you [children] have to listen to are your parents, teachers, law enforcement, and any other person in authority, unless you feel you are in danger. These individuals are adults and if you feel there is a problem, tell the adults who are responsible for you, and let them deal with it. These people are due respect-- if for nothing else than their position alone. This will not just help you today, but for the rest of your life. I cringe sometime when my child tells me about some of the disrespect for authority she has witnessed amongst her peers (that's another story).

Now other than the above-mentioned people, like your peers, strangers, and sometimes even your siblings, you must decide what you will or will not accept. Standing up for yourself can sometimes be as simple as walking away; only fools argue with themselves. If someone says something that you feel is not true, you can either correct them or ignore it; however if it is true, again, acknowledge it or ignore it. Either way there is no need to argue, because who knows the real truth about you and your life better than you and God?

MOST IMPORTANT: THIS IS ONLY THE FIRST PHASE OF YOUR LIFE!

It is only the beginning; start today thinking about the direction you want your life to go in the next phase, after high school- young adulthood.

1. You know what type of situation you live in, but you do not know about the next person.
2. Treat people how you want to be treated.
3. If you run and coward from people now, you will do it the rest of your life.
4. Life is not fair, but still do the right thing.

How easy will this be? Well, that depends on where you are now. All young people have questions about life. Some of these questions should be answered before they are asked: listen to your parents or caregivers. Parents and caregivers, listen to those in your care. Teaching your children what they may encounter on life's journey will help them in their decisions, as they get older. Parents correct them when they are wrong in their thinking or actions. Stand behind them if you know without a doubt they are right, but do not up hold them when they are proven to be wrong. If you do, it is a set up for failure. Let your children know just how special they are every chance you get!

There have been many people who went thru adverse situations who are now tops in their fields. Others who seemed to be destined for greatness ended up at the bottom, never to find their way back up. The very person you look down on today just may be the one who has to save your life 10 years from now. All I'm saying is **be kind to one another starting now and think about the other person before you speak or act**.

# Let's Go to Work

Suppose you go into work one day, and your supervisor pulls you aside to tell you that he will be trading places with you for one day. This is your lucky day- or is it? This is your chance to show management why this job should really be yours! Instead you freak out because you have no idea what your supervisor goes thru in HIS day. On the other hand, your supervisor will have a chance to see just what your day can be like as well.

A machine is only as good as the person who operates it. If the wrong button is pushed, all hell can break loose. Continuous monitoring of the different parts of the machine and addressing problems as they arise will cause smooth operations.

It's the same way in the work place. As a supervisor, it is good to know the jobs of all the people you are responsible for supervising (some knowledge of the person's position you report to is helpful as well). When you know what it takes to do the job, you know what is needed to produce. You should be the spare part. When there is a slowdown in production or a malfunction, you should be able to fill in to insure continued smooth operations. But who will do your job, if you have to step in and do someone else's? YOU! Good supervision will keep all parts functioning so smoothly, that when one part starts to go down, the rest will automatically over compensate. Supervisors should never ask employees to do something they are not willing, ready and able to do themselves.

Think of ways to motivate your employees to want to do a good job. Let those you supervise know how much you appreciate what they do. Compensation can be given in more ways than a paycheck. Hard work is its own reward; however a simple "thank you" or "good job" goes a long way. Cash is always good, but an extra day off or few hours of release time will motivate most people to try harder. Team efforts can be rewarded with a catered lunch or gift certificates.

Weak parts should be worked with. Perhaps put in different ways to try to find a good fit. Every effort should be made to help employees fit in; after all, there was a reason that particular person was chosen to begin with. When all efforts have been made, and the person just will not fit in, you should do what is best for the group as a whole. Anybody can get a job, but it's up to the individual to keep it.

There are some of you, who were actually sought out by employers for a particular job. This gives you a definite advantage. However, unless you were hired after an internship, or volunteer work, all a perspective employer has to go on is your application, an interview, or references. Now you have to produce. If you don't, the employer will just go back into the files and find somebody else who can turn out what he promises.

Getting a job is really not a problem. If you are a high school graduate or have earned a GED, you are employable. This action alone shows you are capable of learning. Discipline and social skills acquired thru this learning process have prepared you to interact with other people. So you get a job, but how do you keep it?

If you are not a morning person, then don't get a day job. If you can't stand to be on your feet all day, then don't apply for a position that requires a lot of standing. If you don't have reliable transportation, make sure you have a way to get to work on time! It is better to be thirty minutes early than thirty minutes late. You should know what is required before you agree to accept the job. If you know over time is required then don't gripe when the time come to do it. If you know a certain dress code is required, don't be offended if you are informed that you are not meeting the requirements. Being a team player is very important. Never say, "That's not my job" when a supervisor ask you to do something extra. Remember they are doing their part to keep the whole operation running smoothly.

Now if the conditions and terms change after you sign on, then you have one of two choices: accept them or find another job. I can guarantee there is somebody out their ready, willing, and able to take your place. After all, chances are they did not come knocking on your door begging you to take the job. Most likely you went to them, which means you can leave whenever you get ready.

Be considerate of others. After all, you know what you go thru when not working, but do you know what the next person goes thru? Don't work overtime unless you are getting paid; in other words, leave work at work. Don't even think about your job or the people on it, unless you get paid to do it. Also, when you go to work, leave your personal life at the door.

Change is often necessary in the work place. Unless it's your company and you sign the paychecks, changes are not your decision to make. When making changes, the people who have to implement the change must be taken into consideration. When change is properly prepared for, it is accepted better and adapted to.

If you are employed in any sector, you should be thankful. Just ask the people who are now looking for a job. Your job may not be perfect, but until you come up with a better idea, you need to make it perfect for you!

# CHANGE

Life is about change. Some changes are inevitable, like growing older. Some changes can be avoided, like a drunk driver causing a fatal car crash. Changes on the job can be good or bad; it mostly depends on the attitude towards the changes to be made. We change as we get older; but at different rates based on education, social-economics, environment, family structure, and this list could go on and on. The outcome depends on the reasons for the change and the attitude of the people required to implement the changes.

Changes made in the life of a child are most likely the decision of someone else. When I decided to move to Henderson, Tennessee from Gary, Indiana, I had the best interest of my children in mind. We would be closer to my family and the environment was totally different. Did my children, who were nine at the time like the change? No, but it was either move to a place that I knew would be safer for their upbringing or make the decision to stay where we were with the dangers (gang recruitment, drug wars, poverty, and….) I knew were ahead. Even though my twins (especially my son) did not like it at the time, he has since thanked me for sticking to my decision. I think parents should make the choices for children under the age of 18.

At 18, the law feels a person is capable of making her own choices, but the parents always have the last say so in what will or will not be accepted in their home; regardless of the age of the child. Children want what they want because they do not have the mental capacity to know what is best for them. Another problem that will arise when children are allowed to do what they want is that there will come a time when they must be told "No". They will not understand the change, which will lead to rebellious defiant behavior. Children grow up. Part of raising children is teaching them how to make good choices and teaching accountability and consequences when they don't. If you are the parent who feels your child can do no wrong; it is always someone else's fault; or someone else made them do it- STOP IT! I have all ways told my children, "You cannot stand before the judge and say- Your Honor 'such and such' made me do it. He has you and you will be the one in trouble!"

One good thing about being an adult is that I do not have to consult with anyone on the choices I make. Now, do I have to take others into consideration? Of course. However, when it's all said and done, the final choice is mine. Sadly, there are some adults who are not free to decide. Women (or men) involved in abusive relationships feel they do not have that freedom because of the repercussions from an intimate partner. Changes of this type can only be made by the individual in that present situation. People stay in abusive relationships for a reason; they grew up in this type of environment so they think it's normal. Others self-esteem has been beaten so low until they feel no one else will want them, and they have no means of support if they do escape. Some even think they can change the abuser.

There are a few things wrong with that logic. First, there are too many agencies available 24 hours a day/7 days a week, ready to assist you out of your situation. Also you are teaching your children (male and female) that it's ok to be mistreated by their partner. Children will often repeat the same behavior when they grow up or they will choose the total opposite; some will be extremely defensive and become an abuser in place of being abused. When it comes to affairs of the heart, change is an individual decision. Only you know when you are sick and tired of being sick and tired! Change in these instances can be horrifying, but you are never alone. If one has faith in God, just the size of a mustard seed, just do it; don't look back and I promise He will lead you in the right direction and cause people to cross your path to aide you on your journey. Just don't forget to tell Him "thank you"!

Change on the job-Oh No! If it ain't broke, why try to fix it? The people you work for are in business to make a profit. In order to turn a profit, they must keep up with or surpass the competition. Any business that does not make changes will not be in business very long. When change comes to your job embrace it as an opportunity for self-growth; the more you know the better off you become. When change presents itself on your job, you have a few choices: one thing you can do is quit-which would be nonsense, unless you have a better opportunity waiting; another thing you can do is whine, complain, or resist the change- then you may be fired. A better alternative is to make it your mission to get the best understanding of how the change is expected to take place and where you fit in the process. Take notes and use them until you get the swing of it. It is not always necessary to know why the changes are needed (unless it's your company), but you do need to understand how and where you fit to make it a success. As long as you do what is required, if it does not go well, it won't be your fault or responsibility.

Another change some face is the role of caring for elderly or sick parents. When my twins were young, I would tell them if they did not behave, I would drop them off at the foster home (we visited often to donate clothes and other items). Well, when they were about 17, we were sitting around talking and my son stated, "That nursing home is looking better and better". When I asked him what he meant, he calmly reminded me of my threat to take them to the foster home! Wow, did I get a revelation! That being said, be very careful how you treat your children, they have to decide how they want to treat you some day!

If you are ever faced with such a decision, consider what is best for the person. You can have the best intentions, but you are not the one who will have to deal with the inadequacies of not being handled by professionals. This can at times cause more harm than good. Get your feelings and concerns of what other people think out of the way. Do what you know is best to make the latter years as comfortable as possible.

# WASTED EMOTIONS

Have you ever found yourself angry, but did not know why? Perhaps people at work or school, getting on your last nerve. The kids seem to have lost their minds: not doing chores, mouthing off –going thru the stage from teen to young adult. Let us not forget the grown children who never left or keep coming back. Then there is the spouse who just doesn't understand; either oblivious to the chaos or happy as long as dinner is cooked and the bills are paid. Your home should be your castle; with one king and/or queen and the rest are servants (for lack of a better word).

The one place a person should have peace is in their home; you pay the cost to be the boss. Work, however, is a different story; unless of course you are the boss. One can only control his (own) behavior and actions. My theory: Usually people who try to run things-say at work, school, church, etc. …. are usually this way because they cannot control the things they need to control or have their say with their spouse, children, or the running of their own lives.

If this type of person is giving you problems on the job, my theory may help you to be more tolerant of such individuals and realize their actions and attitude probably has nothing to do with you personally. I have a couple of suggestions: If one is content with his life, then he can be the sounding board another person needs to get a few things off his chest. Just listen- Do not try to solve the problem for them. Say things like, "I hope it all works out" or "I'll be praying for you", or suggest they think long and hard about the situation and follow their intuition.

Now on the other hand, if you have problems of your own, the last thing you want to do is hear someone else's. Suggestion: Politely tell them," I don't mean any harm" or "I hope you don't take this the wrong way, but I have my own issues, and really don't need to take on yours". Maybe try "for every one complaint you have, I have two more." There are times however, when listening to someone else's issues makes you realize you don't have it so bad after all.

Now as for the children, I have covered that in previous articles, but I will recap: Never strike a child when angry-never ever never! All punishment should be age appropriate; children are never too young to learn right from wrong. Terrible two's will grow into tyrant threes, if boundaries are not established early. Teens and pre-teens are a little different. They only want to worry about boys/girls, electronics, who said what- when –where- and how dare they! Their fingers should have blisters from texting and Instagram, Facebook, Twitter and all those other electronic demons we have let invade our homes. My motto: I give and I will take away.

When you notice changes in your little sweetie, don't just blow it off. Remember the manipulation, isolation, and nasty attitude that makes you give in because you don't want them to be ANGRY with you-STOP- if your child never gets upset with you over something, then something is wrong. This is the time in their lives when one must hold tight, know who their friends are, and freedom is earned by following curfew, doing household chores, etc....

Now I do not agree with kids watching kids; however, if there are things in the house that must be done, and an older sibling has to entertain a younger sibling and you are in eyeshot of them both, then the older child needs to be praised for helping out. If you have a responsible teenager who has to help care for the younger children, I think they should be paid, not as much as an outside sitter or day care, but something to let them know they are appreciated. This can also be a method of birth control; taking care of smaller children can make a teenager more careful not to have her own one too soon (It worked in my house). This should never be a full time job for children, because it will rob them of their own special time to be their real age.

For grown children who do not work, your job is to look for a job until you find one. They cannot sleep until 2 pm, and then go job hunting. If they are helping out and everybody is getting along, then good. But if they are trying to run your home with disrespectful behavior, not following rules set by you, or just basically being a source of tension in your home, they need a time limit to be out on their own. If it means packing their stuff and renting them a room for a couple of weeks or a month, let them know (and you must stand FIRM), it's on them now.

"If momma is not happy, then no one is"; is very true. Most mothers (whether single or married) are the backbone of the family. Each person in the relationship should be appreciated for the part he or she plays. Taking care of the kids, keeping the house clean, and washing the clothes is just as important as making the money to provide for the household. Just try doing all these things while working and having a spouse who feels as though his job is done when he lays the paycheck on the table.

Battles should be chosen carefully; everything is not worth fighting over. Never disagree in front of the children. It can cause them inner stress and can cause them to act out when away from home. Always present a united front, in front of the children; if you don't, they will find a way to work it in their favor, as they get older. Two screaming people never solve anything. Cool off, and then talk it out like adults. Always try to come to a compromise- even if it's to agree to disagree.

Anger is a wasted emotion. If an incident still bothers

you long after it's over, you allow the person you had the problem with to have control over your emotions and they have probably forgotten all about it. Self-pity is also a waste of time; if you don't like your life, and you are of legal age, then it's up to you what you do about it. I remember when my twins were about 18 months old. I called my mom "complaining" about my life and such. She politely told me, "I did not ask to be invited to your pity party" and she hung up on me! If I find my mind headed in that direction now, I have a party of two- the one person who let's me vent and myself; party over real quick. Before I became injured, my punching bag that hung on my carport was the best stress reliever ever! I would think about who ever or whatever had pissed me off as the bag, and beat the crap out of 'em! Have your pity party, then move on.

To minors: you have the rest of your life to make your own choices. Choose wisely, because you will only have yourself to blame. Don't just live, but live and learn. We all have too many mistakes to make in life without making the same mistakes over! Talk about it to a parent, relative, teacher, minister, counselor- SOMEBODY- until someone listens and helps you figure it out. Short answer: Puberty- it will pass! Your brain and your body go through some major changes during this time. Females start to refocus at about 17.5- 18, males about 25 (maybe, if ever).

# Time for a Change

**Re-cid-i-visim**- The tendency to relapse into a previous undesirable behavior, especially crime.
**Recidivist**- A person that is continually in and out of jail for the same crime or something new.
*mala prohibita* - "Prohibited evil"; Term referring to crimes that are wrong primarily because the law declares them to be wrong ( ex. Public intoxication, shoplifting, driving without a license.....)
.
*mala in se*- "Evil in itself"; Term referring to crimes like murder, that are universally condemned.

This article will discuss some of the reasons I feel that people are in and out of correctional facilities and how reduction is possible. If you think this does not affect you, keep reading. I was about 22 years old when I worked at a maximum/medium security correctional facility in Indiana. Some of the women scoffed when they learned my age, feeling how could I tell them what to do when most of them were older than me. My reply was, " Respect me as an officer and I will respect you as an inmate; because the only difference between us was you got caught, and I didn't." In our adult life, most of us have done SOMETHING that we could have been locked up for; knowingly or not; it happened.

What does this have to do with people going back to jail? A lot. What good will it do to not ask the question on a job application, "Have you been convicted of a crime?" Once the background check comes back, you find out without asking, but did not hire the person because of it? When there is a person standing before you who is humbly asking for a fair chance to earn an upright living, to set the best example he can for his children, so he can break the generational curse of poverty, abuse, illegal activity, and social economic depravity that has plagued their family. All they want and need is a chance. This is one of the main reasons [a lack of a job] people recidivate back into the correctional system.

Who are we to judge? Now if the crime was *mala in se*, depending on the job, I could understand the apprehension in considering this person for employment. Other crimes, considered *mala prohibita* are only wrong because the majority of society says so. However, people have paid their debt to society, as set down by the laws of the land. So why is there still such disdain for people who have been given the label of ex-offender? Why does society make it so hard on this person by requiring them to "pay" to stay out of jail? Never mind that this person cannot find a decent job but has to settle for two minimum wage jobs just to support himself; heaven forbid he has a family. It becomes about what it has always been about- doing what one has to do to survive. Am I condoning illegal or immoral behavior? Of course not. I'm saying be careful how you judge other people; but for the Grace of God, it could've been you.

Is society expecting too much? Maybe. During felony incarceration (more than 11 months and 29 days), the sentences can range from 1 year to life in prison. And even though some young people thought they are Billy or Betty Bad Ass on the outside, they find out real quick, it means nothing, because you are now living with the real Billy and Betty Bad Ass. They've got the scares or tattoos to prove it! The number one goal in prison is SURVIVAL. This leaves very little time for rehabilitation-without which, there can be very little if any reform.

Once these people are released back into society, they are expected to do something they have never had to do: hold down a legitimate job, pay bills, refrain from any illegal activity, obtain a valid driver's license, and not to mention, pay all the probation/parole fees, restitution, and other charges put upon them. Okay, what happened to the time one was incarcerated working on a job for less than a dollar a day? It is a set up for failure. Even if one is fortunate enough to get a good job, something he has never had before, how does he know what is expected of him- perhaps 40 yrs old and first one in the family to get a job with benefits.

Most do not come home to a loving family prepared to take care of them while they acclimate back into society. The family also goes thru changes, not fully understanding what they have been thru, and why they act differently.

People cannot do what they do not know how to do. They can have desire, willingness, and determination, but people parish due to lack of knowledge. I hope in the near future to open a counseling center, "Finally A Chance" whose main goal is to help all people live the best life possible, but especially those who never have a chance from the start. For people who suffer from PTSD from the military, prison, abuse, or whatever keeps them from moving forward, we want to be there to help.

## Where Do We Get It From?

How do children learn right from wrong or what is expected of them, as they get older? How do children know if they are being disrespectful to themselves or others; rude for no reason except because they can? What determines the decisions made about our lives and the lives of those under our care? When one is single and has no one to care about but one's self, the decisions are easier. I told my children, when they turn 18, they get to make their own decisions, because if they do what I want, and it does not turn out right, they will blame me; but, if they do what they want, and it does not turn out right, they can only blames themselves. I let them know, I am their number one fan and biggest supporter. I will try to help them as long as they were helping themselves, but they are on their own (In my mind, the age of adulthood is 21). They were also told from a very young age, that if they chose not to go to college or get a trade, then they better get a good job, because I was NOT going to take care of grown ups! I would never try to tell anybody how to raise their children; only what worked for me. See, I felt confident in telling them these things, because from the beginning, I was preparing them to be responsible, productive grownups that could give something back to society.

As soon as I first laid eyes on my babies, one in a pink hat and the other in a blue one, my first thought was, "Now I am responsible for more than myself". I was 25 yrs old and single. Little FYI: the saying "momma's baby daddy's maybe" refers to more than paternity: Daddy may be around-may not. He may provide- may not. May marry you- probably won't, but let's be real; there are way more single mothers in the world than single dads.

As parents, single or not, you must be careful of what is allowed to influence your household. Men can be the biggest influence in a child life. A dad shows a boy how to treat a woman. If he grows up around an abusive male, he will most likely become abusive. If he witnesses his mom accept this behavior, this leads him to believe it's okay. The same boy, who tries to defend his mom as a child, has a better chance himself becoming abusive. However, if he observes the men in his life as respectful of their mothers or wives, going to work, and being a provider, then he will learn how to be a real man. The boy, who grows up doing chores, helping around the house, and watching a productive male, is more likely to develop these same characteristics as an adult.

A girl needs to learn her worth early on. The men in her life show her how a woman should be treated, by how he treats her mom and other women. A mom shows her girls what is acceptable by how she allows the men in her life to treat her. If she does not witness her mom being cursed and disrespected by men, she will not accept it from young men who come into her life. She is taught respect for herself and her body (boys need these lesson as well); she is not witness to everything or person her mom has in her own life, but only those who should have her best interest at heart (dad, granddads, uncles). Kids pick up the temperament, good or bad, from a young age. The behavior is later displayed by how they allow others- first peers, and later partners, to treat them.

Teach your children about "good touch" and "bad touch". This conversation should be age appropriate, begin from the time they are old enough to talk, and continue until the age of consent. Sexual abuse has changed the total direction of many, many lives, and still continues today (that's another issue).

We all come here knowing nothing; we had to learn from

somewhere. Lessons of charity, love, respect, self-control, social skills, and discipline should begin at home and continue throughout life. However, when people are given freewill to run their lives to soon, and without the tools needed (self-control, consequences, accountability, etc....), it is a set-up for a rough road ahead.

## ACT LIKE A LADY AND GET THAT MAN!

Without a doubt, Mr. Steve Harvey really helped a lot of women figure out what they were doing wrong in relationships. It's the one time I regret we are so close in age, because, like most of you, "if I knew then", what Big Brotha Steve has laid out for us now; a lot of our lives would have taken a different turn. Because Brother Steve is four years older than myself, by the time he wrote the book, I had most of the stuff figured out, and actually know a man that reminded me of the good guy in the movie. Steve, I don't want to think like a man (LOL); because in my opinion, all y'all are freaking crazy! But, we were meant to live with each other; and would be really lonesome without you fellas.

Ladies and gentlemen, the 90-day rule is really a good start. But don't look at it as a countdown to jump in the sack; instead, use the time to check this person out in various situations. In times, like around his family, your family; if the waiter pisses him off, or he has some really good "intentions", but months to a year later, he's still "intending". He will make you many promises to get "the cookie", but it will only go as far as it gets. Example: He takes you to dinner and a movie a few times. The conversation is about all the good times y'all will have taking trips or taking you shopping.., but if after a few dates, you give up the "goods"- the trips and shopping will most likely not happen.

God created sex for marriage, between a man and a woman; any sex outside of marriage is wrong; but the marriage bed cannot be defiled. In other words, if you are married, you can do all most any freaky sneaky "thang" you want –with the person you are married too. In the sight of God, it's ok. The problems occur when people take a beautiful thing like sex and use it for their own selfish pleasure. I think it's one of the main reasons the divorce rate is so high-- not to mention domestic abuse, single parenthood, and questions of paternity. If you started messing around with a married person, and they do leave their spouse for you (which is very rare), don't think for one minute they won't do the same thing to you. As a matter of fact, every time they are late, going in another room to answer the phone, and other obvious sneaky behavior, it will be the first thought that comes to your mind. Remember, if they will do it with you; they will do it to you; this applies to men and women.

Relationships have taken a complete turnaround in the

past 20 years. With Internet dating and more women than ever doing it for themselves- not to mention the shortage of Black men due to excessive incarceration- options are very limited. People now come from so many different adverse situations that they manage to keep "crazy" under wraps long enough to appear "normal". Then, all of a sudden, crazy shows up. It's a lot harder to get out of a bad relationship, than into a healthy one. Sex when you are too young to know what's going on, or to immature to make such a life altering decision, or not taking the time to develop a friendship, or intimate relationship before you dive head first into a physical relationship, will most likely end bad. Sexual promiscuity most time starts from being physically mishandled as a child; sometime too young or in ways where they don't even realize when it happened. These issues must be addressed and dealt with, before the person will be able to maintain healthy relationships with others.

Consider your actions in your child eyes; they do not need to know everybody you know. Children have no business in grown-up affairs. In other words, you may think your child is into that video game or movie, and you are close by on the phone just talking away. FYI- that child is listening to everything you say. Then on top of that, when you run into this person, say at church or the grocery store, or PTA meeting, your child may see you act the opposite of how you were just talking about this same person on the phone!

If you are a single parent, do not put down the other parent to the child. Regardless of how you feel about that person, the child still has love for him or her. If they are not as they should be, the child will eventually figure it out. Don't allow anybody to disappoint a child in your care too many times. If you do, the child will develop trust issues that will carry over into adulthood.

It comes down to respect for yourself, your children, and others. It is also important to make other people respect you. Talking to someone for 90 days does not make a relationship. If you are only doing the 90 days on the advice of Mr. Harvey and not using the time to establish a friendship, understanding and solid foundation- why waste your time. You can't holler, "No, no we still got 85 days left"; you just blew it. Some think, I'll string this person along for a few months, "get the drawers", and then move on. Know what you are holding out for or you will be disappointed in the end- again.

I have always told my girls, "Where the last date ends is where the next date will pick up". In other words if the last date got to patting, rubbing, and feeling, that's where the next date will pick back up!

I told my son, "If a girl is throwing the "goodies" at you, chances are she's throwing them at the next man too." Tell her, "My momma warned me about girls like you- get away from me!" Does he do it? I hope at least some of the time, but he is like most other young men; he treats his women friends, just like they act.

Just like a house, the foundation determines whether or not it will stand; so does relationships. Build your relationship on a firm foundation and you will weather any storm. Build it out of pre-fabricated material, and once the first good storm comes, it will fold.

I love Steve Harvey just like everybody else with any sense. He is inspiring, motivated, and sincere in his faith. Ladies when you make that list of what you want in a man, make sure you are that type of woman!

Remember, if you act like a lady, you will get that man.

Not sure what to do? Read Proverbs 31:10-31. Short version: A real man wants a woman who can bring something to the table. A woman wants a man that can build that table and put something on it!

## Let's Get Married- THEN WHAT?

Spring is in the air, flowers are blooming, everything is green again and of course summer will be here before we know it. Graduation celebrations are planned, long awaited summer get- a-ways are near, and biggest one of them all- WEDDINGS! But, what about the MARRIAGE; how much time and discussion has been spent on what will be required to keep the two of you as one? There are numerous scriptures in the Bible on marriage: the role of the husband, as well as the role of a wife, the rearing of children, and the responsibility of a God fearing, Christian household. If you want an honorable God fearing husband, Proverbs 31:10-31 lets you know the type of woman you should strive to be. Attitudes, habits, and behaviors do not change with the placing of a ring on the appropriate finger, the signing of a legally binding contract, or even a sacred vow taken before God and witnessed by man.

First of all, how well do you REALLY know the person you are about to marry? I was once told one should witness a person in all seasons before getting too serious. Ok, what is the difference between a person in winter and fall? Answer: A person during spring and summer. One should notice the person's intended actions and reactions in all situations. If one is easily agitated, this can be a sign of impatience; this can lead to unnecessary embarrassing situations later on. Of course no one wants a push over, but patience (tolerance of incompetent people) is a sign of maturity and social etiquette. A passive person on the other hand, can be easily manipulated and thus have a hard time gaining and maintaining the respect they deserve.

Does the person you plan to wake up with every morning have a habit of partying all night (drinking, hanging with friends or family), sleeping all day- working when they can; but, don't care when they can't, or a compulsive obsessive workaholic? A ring is not a house arrest bracelet that will make this person stay at home or by your side like you may expect a spouse to do. Signing a piece of paper does not make a person responsible over night. One may start off with the best intentions; intentions and actions are two different things. If these have been issues of concern during courtship, it may be best to witness this transformation from the person one has --to the spouse one wants.

If this love of your life, the one you feel you cannot be

without makes you laugh and oh so happy great, but....FYI- My mom says "the one that makes you laugh, may also make you cry". Also, "anybody can be on his best behavior for a little while." All couples should have an understanding of their intended views on family roles, religion, politics, education, child rearing, household chores, financial responsibility, etc... Although you may not agree, sometimes things are open for negotiation, compromise and resolution; where as some things can be deal breakers. Know some history: criminal background, unresolved childhood/family issues, and work history. These are real issues that can have an impact on ones future and family. It is wise to receive Biblically based pre-marital counseling, either from a Minister or a Certified Biblical Counselor. There will still be trial and error, but at least you will have a reference point.

Ephesians 5:24-25 Therefore as the church is subject unto Christ, so let the wives be to their own husband in everything. [25] Husbands, love your wives, even as Christ also loved the church, and gave himself for it.

Simply put- Wives if your husband puts you first, after God, is protective, providing to the best of his ability, and professes his love for you by being faithful, honest, and respectful; you should have no problem consulting him in anything that will in any way have an affect on the family. Husbands, this position is earned not just given; if you do not get this type of respect from your wife, then you may want to check yourself first. Wives, if you have this type of husband, then remember-what it took to get him is what it will take to keep him.

Marriage, like rearing children is one of the hardest jobs in the world. Marriage is like a career; the longer one is in it, the more rewarding, comfortable, and fulfilling it should become. Child rearing is a job; you should eventually retire, but keep in touch, because one will be missed if they don't.

# Random Act of Kindness

People do not have to be nice to you; but it is nice to be nice; we should all be kind to one another. One of my rules for contentment is to treat others how I want to be treated. However, I learned a long time ago not to expect the same thing in return; it's a set-up for a letdown. A random act of kindness is to do something for someone just because an opportunity presents itself.

An example would be if you are in line at the store, and you notice the person behind you only has one or two items, in comparison to your basket full, it would be an act of kindness to let that person go ahead of you. Or in this same situation, ask the cashier to ring up that person purchases with your own (yes, it does happen, because it happened to me and I have also did it for others). It gives a good feeling to both the giver and the receiver; it's sometimes best if done to a stranger, this way you both know there is no hidden agenda.

Helping someone that you know is in need, but too proud to ask for help is a show of kindness. This can be done by suggesting maybe a yard sale or bake sale, AND then help get it organized. To offer a solution without the willingness to help see it thru is a waste of time. A person tells you of a family in the neighborhood who has fallen on hard times and cannot buy groceries because they had nothing left after paying the light bill, and you say something like "bless their heart" and then go on your way. You just missed the mark; it is not their heart that needs to be blessed, but their pockets!

A young man once asked me for a couple of dollars because he was hungry and just wanted a couple of burgers from McDonald's. My first thought was this is a growing boy and a couple of burgers are not going to be enough. So instead, I took him to the grocery store and spent about $25 so the household had enough food for the rest of the week.

A person once told me a true blessing is to do something for somebody without the person knowing where it came from. This is so true, because instead of getting the glory for you, hopefully they will thank God for the blessing and the person He used to deliver it. I have done this on a few occasions; why? It's a blessing to be a blessing to others. In my opinion, God will increase what you have when you learn to use it to help others. If you have a lot of money, but afraid to help another person, you will loose it, with no idea of where it went. One the other hand, if you help other people, you will always have plenty.

I have a few guidelines for myself: The Bible tells us not to lend more than we can afford to lose. I'd rather give you what I can afford, instead of lending you what I know you cannot pay back. I cannot help everybody, nor do I help the same person over and over again. I cannot help anyone who is not trying to help himself; this goes for family, friends, and foes (strangers). I do not look for returns from others. All my blessings are from above. Do not help people just to get something back or with regret; help them because you can. All help is not monetary; a kind word or gesture goes just as far.

# BE THANKFUL

The Holiday Season has begun! We all have more to be thankful for than we realize. We take the little things for granted, like breathing, walking, a reasonable amount of health and strength, and the ability to take care of the basic necessities of life. No matter your situation in life, it could always be worse. So in all things-GIVE THANKS!

If you have a home, no matter the size or location, that's something to be thankful for; just ask the person who slept outside last night. Of course we don't have that problem in Chester County, but there are some that are staying with others, because they have no other choice. One would not have to travel far to find families living in their car or on the street. If what you have is not what you want, be thankful and take care of it from your heart, like it is just what you want, and watch what happens. If your automobile gets you from point A to point B, then be thankful. Again, if you want better, cherish what you have and watch what happens.

Most of us hang out with family and friends during the holiday season; most ill will and disagreements are set-aside in honor of the holiday to "give thanks". If you are truly thankful, but still holding a grudge, why pretend? "He who searches the heart also knows the mind." True forgiveness is not something that one picks up and put down. True forgiveness is from the heart and removes the sting from whatever the problem was. It is not always easy, but each person should consider some of the things God has forgiven you for- never to be remembered again.

We cannot pick our family, but we have to love and accept them any way. Life is short and once a person has left this world, one no longer has the chance to make it right. So take this time to forgive others, thus freeing your self.

Do you have a job? Then, be thankful. Just consider somebody who has not worked in a couple of years, but has a family to support. With all the changes being made and the economic situation of this country, no job is secure. Some of us, while thankful for whatever source of income we attain, know that God is our provider, and His resources are unlimited. This leads me to my next point-Christmas; the true reason for the season.

Friday after Thanksgiving it was on and popping! The crowds, the bargains, stores staying open late, people in a frenzy trying to find that perfect gift. NEWS FLASH- The perfect gift has already been given. He was born in a manger, outside of an Inn in Bethlehem; his name is Jesus, the Son of God. With this gift comes love, peace, joy, and good will towards all man. People have not always had money and credit; before lay-a-way and stores full of toys and gadget, gifts were handmade and from the heart. Children were happy with some candy and a piece of fruit or a handmade doll- anything new.

Consider this- Make a list of the people you usually buy a gift for (put family members of the same household together). One of my favorite things to do is find a photograph and have it framed and enlarged with effects- or framed just like it is. This takes thought, because you will pick a picture that is a memory you know is special to them. Baked goods are always in order. I have cousins who remind me every year how they are not happy about me ending a Christmas tradition of giving my homemade cookies as gifts. It gave me great joy to bake those cookies, sometime all day and again a week later; several times until Christmas. I would give these cookies to my family, co-workers, and anybody I considered a friend or acquaintance. The direction for these cookies was right on the bag, with one exception, the main ingredient- LOVE.

*Think about the person, use your imagination, and give from the heart. Whether it is handmade or store bought, these same principles can apply; save some time, energy, frustration and money.*

Nothing dampens my spirit more than to run across a child (old or young) who can only tell what they RECEIVED for Christmas and not what they GAVE. We received the GREATEST gift that will ever be given on this sacred day over 2000 years ago; and there will never be any greater! So, please make sure the people you are responsible for know the real reason for the Christmas season. Tell the children, because of the birthday of the baby Jesus, we celebrate the day, named after him, Christmas. It is a day of giving AND receiving love and good cheer to all.

I wish God's blessing for each and every one of you during this Christmas season and all God has for you in this upcoming New Year!

# ONENESS

## A LETTER TO NEWLYWEDS

WHAT GOD HAS JOINED TOGETHER, LET NO MAN
SEPARATE.
ONENESS IS THE THREE OF YOU TOGETHER THAT WILL
WEATHER ANY STORM.
ONENESS IS WHAT WILL ALLOW YOU TO WAKE UP
EACH MORNING THINKING WHAT I CAN DO TO MAKE
THIS PERSONS DAY BETTER.  ONENESS IS WHAT WILL
NOT ALLOW YOU TO REST WHEN YOUR SPIRITS HAVE
BEEN AT ODDS FOR MOST OF THE DAY.
ONENESS WILL ALWAYS MAKE YOU LOOK 25 IN EACH
OTHER'S EYES WHEN YOU GET TO BE 65!!!
ONENESS IS THE TWO OF YOU SO INTERTWINED WITH
EACH OTHER, THAT EVEN WHEN YOU ARE PHYSICALLY
APART, YOU WILL STILL FEEL THE CLOSENESS.
A MAN SHALL LEAVE HIS MOTHER AND FATHER AND
HE SHALL CLEAVE TO HIS WIFE, AS THE TWO ARE NOW
ONE.
AS LONG AS YOU KEEP THE ONLY ONE WHO IS ABLE TO
COMBINE TWO PEOPLE AND KEEP THE TWO PHYSICAL
BEINGS IN ONE SPIRIT;
THAT THIRD PERSON;
A COMBINATION OF BOTH YOU AND HIM,
NO MAN WILL BE ABLE TO SEPARATE.

# A TRIBUTE to My TWINS
## JAMISON and JUMESE MCCAIN-CLARK

I have a set of twins: a girl and boy who turned 26 on the 26th of January 2014.  When they turned 21, I did not have money to buy them a gift, so, I decided to give them 21 pieces of advice. These were some of the things they had been taught all their lives. The law says, once people turn 18, they are considered adults. They can fight in a war, but not buy liquor. I cannot have access to certain information, but whenever a problem arises, I am the first one they would (and still do) call. I try not to tell them what to do, but offer my advice, and let them know the final decision is theirs to make. When they turned 18, I told them it was time for them to make their own decisions, because if they did what I wanted, and it didn't go right, they would blame me. However, if they did what they wanted to do, and it did not go as planned, they could only blame themselves. I informed them that I was their number one fan, biggest supporter, and would have their back; but basically, they were on their own. I had no intentions of really cutting the apron string until they were 21. I want to share with you, some of the advice I gave to them.

1. Keep God first.

2. Be kind to strangers; you never know when you may be entertaining an Angel.

3. Treat people how you want to be treated.

4. Always respect authority.

5. Stay humble; remember ALL our help comes from the Lord.

6. If you make a mistake, admit it, and move on.

7. If you learn something from the mistake, then it was a not a mistake, but an experience.

8. There are too many mistakes in this life to make, to make the same ones over again.

9. To your own self always be true.

10. You have from the time you think about doing wrong, until the time you actually do it, to change your mind.

11. Try not to act on impulse.

12. If you act on impulse; proceed with caution.

13. Never be afraid to ask for help.

14. Never assume; always ask if you are not sure.

15. Always be able to provide for yourself.

16. If a person asks you a question, their actions will be based on your response. So, if you are not sure then say so!

17. In all things, get an understanding.

18. You can always learn something new from anybody.

19. You will never know everything (mainly my son).

20. Pick your battles carefully; most things are not worth the fight.

21. Give an honest day's work, for an honest day's pay; and always work like somebody is watching.

22. Trust in the Lord with all your heart, and lean not to your own understanding. In all your ways (good, bad and indifferent) acknowledge Him and He will direct your path. Proverbs 3:5-6.

Do they follow this advice? Thankfully most of the time; but if not, at least I know they know it. And I must say, so far, so good. I thought once they were grown and on their own, my life would get easier. In a way it has, but man can it get expensive. I am very proud of my twins, because they are wild, BUT respectable, knowledgeable, productive people, with good hearts and strong minds. I have my daughter home now TEMPORAILY and the Lord knows I needed her for just a little while. My son is over 500 miles in distance, but only a phone call away. For this I am very thankful. HAPPY 26TH BIRTHDAY JAMISON AND JUMES, I LOVE YOU, AND THANK GOD FOR YOU!!!!

TO GLENNA E. GREEN:

HAPPY BIRTHDAY TO MY BABY!
(They truly broke the mold after this one)

On May 19th of this year (2014), my baby turned 17.

While I have been waiting for her to grow up so I can "be free";

my first two are showing me, I will never ever be free of none of

'em as long as we are all alive. I now realize, that's a good thing. I

looked forward to my twins growing up and leaving home; but

they came back! ☺. It's not a bad thing, because I am glad for

them to have a home to come back too. However, the older they

are, the more space they take up. And whether they like it or not-

House Rules (I am the House). Thankfully my oldest daughter is

home for a while; God truly knows best.  But, back to Miss

Glenna, my Diva, Baby, and Fashon-ista ! Now as it gets closer to

that time, I'm not sure if I will be ready in another year. My girls

are 9 yrs apart, and Jumese had Jamison, but Glenna-she is blazing

her own trail. She definitely has enough personality and attitude to

share.

Glenna is my baby and she is a brat (close as allowed)!

One of the many things I admire about Glenna is that she knows of the Spirit that dwells within her; and she does the right thing (as far as I know). I am thankful for the change that has taken place in me over the past 7 years or so. I have an illness that does not tolerate stress; so I keep it to a minimum. That is not always easy with a teenager in today's generation; they seem to have a sense of entitlement. This has been the biggest battle we have had. If Glenna had her way she would have more than her ears pierced and be on her third tattoo by now. Every parent is different, but, I am not going to let my minor child make a decision that will effect the rest of her life. Just like the other two, when she is grown and taking care of herself, I will have no say so. If it goes wrong, she can only blame herself.

Imagination? This girl has enough of that to go around as well. There were times when I had to go out late at night and she would ride with me. We would be riding along and she would mention one of her plans for the future that she knows would get my attention. When I questioned her, the response would be "let me live in the moment". Needless to say, that would then make it funny! She often mentions some life plans that are so far out there; I think it's just to get a reaction out of others. I sure hope I am not around if that imagination comes to life; she is too funny! I told Glenna when she gets frustrated with people, she can think anything she wants; just be careful of what she says out loud. I get to hear not only what she says, but she also shares hers thoughts and dreams; for that, I am thankful.

When Glenna was 8 months old, I went to work at FHU. After two weeks in day care, she got a diaper rash and my mother became the babysitter. It stayed that way until she was old enough to come home with the other children after school. She became well known around town- "the little girl that wears the hats". She also became a "nurse" at a young age. She helped my mother take care of an elderly friend, Mrs. Jones, for as long as she (Glenna) can remember. She also went along when she had to take another elderly friend, Mrs. Mildred to the doctor. About age 6 or 7, she became the nurse of our very dear friend and neighbor, Mrs. Vercie Mae. Glenna took her duties really serious. In Mrs. Vercie's eyes, she could do no wrong. Glenna would comb her hair, polish her nails, just sit and talk her ears off, or watch T.V.

If Glenna was not on the trampoline (she learned how to jump before she could walk), she would be next door. Where did that sweet little girl go? Now she likes to pretend like she's shy; but she has been talking since before she was a year old. While she is not selfish, she can be a little self-centered at times (one of her "moments" was wanting a statue erected in her honor). I mean, what teenager doesn't think the world resolves them (just keeping it real.) I am so thankful Glenna showed her compassionate side early on, because I know it's in her (I wonder sometimes.).

I love my lil Glenna bear☺. I would have been lost had she not been here when the twins were gone. She became my riding buddy; next thing I knew, she's the driver and I'm the rider! Wow, how times flies. Be careful what you wish for; it may come just a little too soon. As I wish my baby, Miss Glenna E. Green, a HAPPY 17TH BIRTHDAY, and know that I wish you many, many, many more!

Baby, you are about to come up on what can be the best time of your life; keep listening to that inner spirit, trust in God, and always push ahead because the sky is the limit. I can't think of another teenager I would want other than you! And when it comes to taking care of me, your experience speaks for itself. Remember, you turned 17 not 18, so I don't need to tell you when to be home!

Things My Momma Told Me

My mom will be 80 yrs old on September 28, 2014. She is a wonderful woman: mother of five girls, nine grandchildren, and eight or nine great- grand's. I thank God for her every day. I call her most mornings, unless she calls me first. If I wait too late in the morning, she has probably already left home (Hot Rod Hanna). As I think of how much I love my mom, for more reasons than I can name, I want to share some of the things she told me over the years that have helped shape me into the person I am today.

- ❖ Don't make fun of people, because you don't know their story; instead say God Help'em.
- ❖ "Trust in the Lord with all your heart; and lean not to your own understanding. In all thy ways acknowledge Him, and He shall direct thy path (Proverbs 3:5-6). I heard these words when things didn't go like I thought they should have as a young adult. However, it was not until I became grown, at the lowest point in my life, and had

nobody else to trust- that I put those words to action in my own life and the life of my children.

❖ Don't advertise what you're not selling. Meaning- too much cleavage and thigh was not needed.

❖ You can't take people ways away from them; what else do they have? This was my first lesson in accepting people as they are. However, If I don't particularly care for a person or situation, I will check myself first (another thing she told me when I would complain), if I feel I am in order, I can remove myself from the situation. You cannot control the actions of others, only your own.

❖ Once I told her, seems like every time I am about to break even or get ahead, something else pops up. She told me, "You have your faith in the wrong thing. You are relying on your paycheck instead of the One who allows you to make a pay check". Those words changed my life. God is my provider!

- ❖ So as a man thinketh, so is he. Nobody knows the heart and the mind of a person, except God.
- ❖ "God is still in control" is what she says when we discuss the affairs of the world.
- ❖ Be consistent and see it through when punishing the children, or else they won't take you serious.

My mom taught me to fear God, and respect other people. She is a very giving person and will help who ever she can. To know her is to love her. Very rarely do I remember her saying a harsh word about anybody; and, it would be difficult to find anybody who can say a bad word about her. Make no mistake, my mom is no pushover. I want to be just like her when I grow up!

Love you Ma, and thank God for you. HAPPY HAPPY HAPPY EIGHTIETH BIRTHDAY to my mother, Mrs. Boytha G. McCain.

# REFLECTIONS

This is a selection of reflections of certain Biblical life applications from my Romans & Galatians class. I hope they inspire you to keep pushing. Try doing some self reflection; you will be surprised where reflections on self will take you.

August-2007 to Dec-2007

## 1.    How does God's grace apply to me?

Almost 2 years ago (August 2005), I was involved in an automobile accident. I was off work for two months; I had just bought the house we had lived in for 9 years, one month prior. My job had no short-term disability at the time, so my income was less than a third. I had heard a Bible study lesson on God's grace. I learned when you go through hard times, if you trust in God, His grace will be sufficient to meet your needs. I tried it- and it worked! My faith increased more from the whole experience.

I have since learned those are "valley experiences". It's when we are in the valley, that the Lord will reach down to pick us up. BUT, not until His work in us is done.

## 2.    How has going to church influenced my life?

I always went to church as a child- whether I wanted to or not. It was during the hard times as an adult that I was more out spoken about God's blessings towards me. Even as a child, I was not ashamed because it was more of a shame if you did not belong to a church. Now I witness to people every chance I get; bail bond clients, friends, family, even strangers! Through the Bible classes I have taken and the memory verses (50 in every bible class) I have learned, the Word of God has become more a part of me. If a scripture I know fits a particular situation, I won't hesitate to use it.

### 3.       Being filled with the Holy Spirit……..

I went through an experience by trusting the wrong person. When it was all over, and no harm had come to me and my children, I was so THANKFUL. I asked the Lord, "What can I do to show You how much I appreciate You seeing me through?" I heard a whisper in my ear that said, "Get closer to me". I started going to church, Sunday school, and Bible study religiously! I studied my Bible with a hunger. When talking to other people, I would find myself quoting scriptures. I told my mom, "I hate to seem like I'm trying to be so "holy", but the Word of God will fit almost any situation people find themselves in."

### 4.       God's Providence

When I was blessed to be able to purchase the house we had lived in for 9 years, I was truly thankful. However, the only way the agency would loan me the money was if I borrowed enough to bring the house up to date (new floors, doors, windows, A/C unit......). Well, this was good too, but it meant EVERYTHING would have to be moved out. During the time my son, who was 16, was in Job Corps and I was divorced; so this left me with my two girls-16 and 7, to do the work. It seemed the more we packed and threw away, the more it was to move! It became very over whelming. Well one night I cried out to the Lord and told Him, "I NEED HELP and some STRENGTH!" The next day when I met my workout partner at 6 a.m., I told her what was going on. She offered to keep my 7 year old for a few days until I was done (He's working it out). Then I mentioned to somebody that I needed tables. They told me the University, where I was working at the time, would let employees borrow tables, deliver and pick them up when done

(WORK IT LORD!). Then, it came to mind that some of the things I was trying to get out of the house could wait until my son; who was coming home in about a week, could take care of. God provided all I needed in people, places, and things I needed to make it happen. Needless to say, anytime I think about having a yard sale, I break out in hives. And end up donating the items.

**5.     Job says if we can praise God during the good times, we must praise Him when times are bad.**

That is so true. When we go through bad times, we must remember God is still in control. I have learned that if I give Him praise when things are not going as I would like, it makes it easier to deal with. "Because we know all things work for the good for those who love the Lord and are called for His purpose" (Romans 8:28). My mom told me during one of the hardest times in my life (pregnant with twins, single and alone): "What don't kill you, will make you stronger". No truer words had ever been spoken to me. I know how to praise God when things are good and even more when they are not so good, because I know He is working it out for me. While we are busy trying to figure it out; God has it already worked out. If you pray; don't worry. If you are going to worry; don't pray.

**6.     God gave them over…..**

I was raised in the church. If there was a service going on, we were there (we lived next door to the church building). In my family, once we turned 18, we had a choice; I chose not to go every Sunday. But looking back, I guess that's why it was easier to do the things I knew were not right. Going to church gives you a remembrance of who God is and how He wants us to live. But the less you go to church, the less you think about it. It is a change; this is also the "regression of sin". However, by being raised in the church, I never strayed so far that I could not find my way back.

### 7.    Interpreting with an Agenda

I have often said, I am very grateful for the church I grew up in. We were taught how to study the Bible and learn of God's purpose for obeying His word. The seeds were planted at a young age. As I grew older, around 9 or 10, the more it made sense, and I knew I wanted Eternal Life; all my sins were forgiven because God gave His Son. This stayed with me as I grew older and became more exposed to the world. Sometimes not having a "true" belief of who God is makes it easier for one to be converted to a different belief: cults are a god example. No matter how someone tries to interpret God's word, I am thankful for my upbringing, and that I have the wisdom and knowledge to interpret for myself!

## 8. Female preachers in the Church

While I do not have a problem with female preachers, I do not think a woman should be the leader of a Church congregation. God intended for man to be the head of the family; I feel the church family is included. Women can read and understand God's word just like men. We may have different ways of getting a message across, but you can learn from anybody who has something to teach.

## 9. Tribulation → Preservation → Character→ Hope

One thing I have learned about trials and tribulations is "stuff" happens to the best of us, but how you handle it determines how you come through. I have learned to be patient and just wait on the Lord. Because while we are worrying about it, God had already worked it out; in His own time it will be revealed. Every adversity should bring about some type of change. Everything I have been through -good, bad, and indifferent, has made me the person I am today. Every situation has bought me closer in my relationship with Christ. And all my experiences have taught me as long as I remember Proverbs 3:5-6 and Romans 8:28, that I know it is all good- COUNT IT ALL JOY !

**10.    Is it amazing grace or trust and obeying that saves us?**

I think it's both. If we trust God's word and live accordingly by obeying, then we will be saved. But no matter how we try, we all fall short (Romans 3:23). Because of God's Amazing Grace and Mercy, every day that we wake up, He gives us another chance to get it right.

**11.    Romans 8:26 Likewise the spirit also helps in our weakness, for we do not know what we should pray for as we ought, But the spirit Himself makes intercessions for us with groaning which cannot be uttered.**

This reminds me that God, in all His infinite wisdom thought of everything. Only He could know that I would not be able to express myself in word or thought. The Heavenly Father knows me better than I know myself. He can read my tears; even when I have no idea why I am crying. I know if all I can do is moan- He knows why. Even in those occasions when we feel good and content for no particular reason, He knows how we got there.

## 12. How can we ask for something in faith that we don't think God will change?

God never changes; He is the same yesterday, today and forevermore…..

"Prayers delayed do not mean prayers denied".

## 13. He is the potter; we are the clay.

Once, my sister and I were having a discussion on raising children. She believes that children should be given a choice in most instances. I feel once they turn 18, they have a lifetime to make choices; until then, the choices are limited. I told her that is why they are called "children" because they do not have enough knowledge to know what is best. If they are given too much "say so" when young, they have a hard time understanding when you say "no". I also told her, to me, children are like clay; you have to shape and mold them, and sometimes pound them into the type of adult you want them to be. You must start when they are young; the more out of shape they become, the harder it becomes to get them back in shape. That also applies to us as Christians; God must shape and mold us by His Grace and Mercy and through His words.

I hope you enjoyed reading this book as much as I enjoyed putting it together. Life goes on, and I will always have something to say. Feel free to contact me at askmeanything731@yahoo.com. Or visit my webpage askmeanything731.wix.com/finallyachance.

Thank you so much and may God bless you all.

## Acknowledgment

I want to acknowledge all my friends and family that knew I could do this long before I did. Momma, thank you for being my biggest fan and supporter. To my children, Jamison, Jumese and Glenna, who will always have to deal with the madness; for which there is a method; it's just who I am. To my oldest and dearest friends, LaRhonda, and Gretchen who has been on me to do this for the past ten years, thanks for being my test client, sounding board, and keeping it 100%. Larry, thanks for the inspiration and encouragement. Dr. Thornthwaite, thanks for showing me the importance of a good education. Those not mentioned by name, are in my heart.

In memory of my good friend Jeffrey "Jeff" Kneeler

December 10, 1957-June 12, 2014

R U M

42319345R00055

Made in the USA
Charleston, SC
21 May 2015